Howard Lull

LEADERSHIP LESSONS LEARNED

HOWARD LULL

Copyright © 2007 Howard Lull

All rights reserved.

ISBN-9781797547947

This book is dedicated to all who desire to be the best leader they can be, and have taken the time to pay the price necessary in development of their professional lives and the investment they are making in the lives of others. Leaders—Listen, Learn and Lead!

ACKNOWLEDGEMENTS

I desire to acknowledge all of the leaders who have invested in my life and have helped me to earn the success I have desired. They are Historical figures as well as many unknown leaders who took the time to acknowledge my potential. I acknowledge God who is the God above all creation and the true leader of leaders, who has been leading people since the beginning of time itself. Many nations turn to him for guidance and leadership when faced with problems too great for any one person. I do as well. I also desire to acknowledge Peter Honsberger CEO of Cold Tree Press and his leadership in making this book successful and leading me through the publishing business. Peter's sincere interest in all his authors is a joy to experience. His expertise in design is second to none. Thanks Peter!

I give a special thank you to all of my family, friends and colleagues who have invested in my life. Well done! I hope I have made you proud. I love you all!

CONTENTS

	Acknowledgments	4
1	Leadership Is Learned	9
2	Leadership Is Imparted	16
3	Leaders Have a Vision	21
4	Leaders Have a Presence	25
5	Leaders Develop Intangibles	28
6	Leaders Work Themselves Out of a Job	32
7	Leaders Exhibit Self Control	35
8	Leaders See and Hear Things	38
9	Leaders Have Followers	41
10	Leaders Are Servants	44
11	Leaders Make Those Around Them Better	47
12	Leaders Hold Themselves Accountable	50
13	Leaders Give Permission	53
14	Leaders Work to Become Leaders	57
15	Leaders Create High Quality Environments	60
16	Leaders Look to Improve Their Effectiveness	63
17	Leaders Perform Self Assessment	66
18	Leaders Lead People and Manage Situations	69

19	Leaders Respond When Caught Off Guard	72
20	Leaders Have a Personal Plan	75
21	Leaders Surround Themselves with Strong People	78
22	Leaders Know the Rules is There Aren't Any Rules	81
23	Leaders Are Loyal	84
24	Leaders Are Givers Not Takers	87
25	Lessons Learned The Hard Way	90
	Final Words	95
	Overview	98

Chapter 1
LEADERSHIP IS LEARNED

Leadership and Learning are Indispensable to each other."
—John F. Kennedy

I know we have all heard that there are born leaders. I don't know about you but I haven't seen one yet. All I have ever seen born is a baby. I have never seen anyone born into maturity. That may sound absurd but I intend to address what others don't say as well as what others falsely say. There is no such thing as a natural born leader. There are, however, people who have personalities and dispositions that incline them toward being a leader. Nonetheless, they too have to learn the lessons and what it takes to be a leader. I have seen tall leaders, short leaders, and leaders in wheelchairs. There are male leaders and female leaders alike who have learned what it takes to be the leader they personally desire. They go through the experimentations and the fires of life to refine their skills and become truly seasoned leaders. That is necessary for us as well. Prepare yourself to learn and then impart your wisdom to others.

I was watching a movie one time where a lady stopped the main character and said, "The world gets out of the way of a person who knows where he is going." The truth in that statement is that people get out of the way of a true leader when they know where the leader is leading them. You, as a leader, have to know where you are heading. If you don't know it, then keep moving forward until it comes into view for you. As a leader, you will have times when people get in the way and cause you distractions. Ignore them and persevere onwards. They may get out of the way, but they may throw you a few challenges you weren't prepared for. Deal with those challenges with integrity. Now, let's look at some ways leadership is learned.

Leadership is learned by observing.

Rarely do I find leaders who are willing to take the time and energy to teach us as they lead us in life. There are many demands placed on leaders today and they don't often have the time to stop and make the necessary investments to pass on their expertise. Therefore, it is up to us to be willing to observe and learn what techniques they use to make their teams and organizations successful. There isn't any one way to be the best leader. I have learned that throughout history, different types of leadership are necessary in different times and situations, just as they are in our world today. Just observe and write notes on the characteristics that were good in which situations and file them for your own future use. I want to point out that it is just as important to realize what didn't work as what did work.

Sometimes we disregard things because they had a bad result. We judge the leader as failing. The truth is we will all fail at times. Leaders just do their failing in front of everyone. Remember that, before passing judgment when you witness someone else fail. I have leaders in my life and I have witnessed their failure. Then when I saw them recover by discovering what it was their team needed them to be, I congratulated them and told them how great it was. I noticed they were appreciative of it, even if they didn't always acknowledge my thoughts. I could see it in their eyes.

We all have stories we can tell of leaders who have failed us. We observe them letting us down morally, financially, through a lack of integrity, and in many other ways. Leaders will fail, but it is how you handle your failure that will ultimately determine your success.

Remember that leadership is learned. Learning by observing is a purposeful event. It is not like sitting in the classroom half asleep, listening to a lecture as we drool in boredom. It is an engagement of all of our faculties and taking notes mentally as well as spiritually. Sometimes it just doesn't feel right. That's being in touch spiritually. All good leaders who observe will develop the spiritual side as well. They will develop the so-called "gut instinct" or "spirit instinct." Having that sixth sense developed is priceless. Strive to learn it, because you can trust your spirit.

Leadership is also learned by experimenting.

As I mentioned earlier, not everything works as planned. I have entered leadership meetings thinking that what I had planned was just what we needed; only to have to change it midcourse because the team was verbalizing other needs to me, and I had to meet those needs before I could get them to the place where I needed them to be. That's not failure. Failure would have been sticking to my original plan and not being sensitive to the needs of my employees. Experimenting is like adding salt to your meal. Salt is a spice that seasons whatever it touches. Salt is made up of sodium chloride. Both sodium and chloride are poisonous if used separately. However, when mixed in the right combination they add a different character to just about anything they are applied to. You learn what seasons a team at the right time. When experimenting I do suggest that you don't go so far in either direction that you leave yourself unable to recover should the need arise. If at any time in your experimenting you realize you are heading towards a disaster, then drop it immediately. Good leaders are not stubborn. They consciously choose the issue for which they will die. Don't die on an insignificant issue or out of ignorance.

I have lead teams in the smallest of hospitals and the largest of hospitals and I have lead teams in hospital systems. All in all, as a leader, I have learned that what works in one place will not necessarily work in another. Not every team is on the same level or in the same stage as others. Some may require intense hands on leadership and others may require a more hands off approach, i.e.

getting out of their way so that they can accomplish what they need to accomplish. Let me give you a sports example. I have seen NFL quarterbacks who felt confined by a coach's inability to allow them to be the athletes that they were. Forced to fit into a system that they feel confines them, they feel underutilized and underappreciated and they also feel that they could win more if allowed the freedom to use their natural skills mixed with their newly learned schemes to be successful. I have seen their coaches fail as they confined them. A true leader releases their people to be successful in the way that only they can, but only if it will lead to both the team's and the organization's success. True leaders desire the team's success above their own. Leaders have long known that stubbornness is not an attractive tool. Don't be afraid to change if necessary.

Leaders learn by questioning.

It is OK to question and to be questioned. It is not OK to be leaders who drill with question after question. If we are alert, we will learn that most of the time our questions are answered as we continue to observe. I have witnessed leaders doing things I totally disagreed with. I was angry they would act like they did, or said what they said, or made the decisions they made. What I learned though, was that after a period of time and removing myself from the situation as a critic, and continuing more as an observer, I finally understood why they did what they did. Only then did it make sense to me. When I am emotionally involved, it doesn't always make sense. When you observe you don't have to be emotionally involved. I suggest though, that you always be objectively involved. In questioning, you may also question yourself as a leader. Questioning and second-guessing are very different things. I see many leaders who don't second-guess themselves. I find that the older and more experienced I get the less I allow myself to second-guess. That's not to say I don't ask myself questions like what could I have done different. I just don't kick myself as hard as I used to when I fail or when I wish could have said or done something different. If you meet a leader who says they have never failed, turn and run from them as fast as you can.

Please note that questioning is not a matter of weakness. I still ask questions to which I know the answer. I like to see if others have answers, or perspectives, that I may not have considered. I recommend you develop a lifetime of learning attitude. If you have already arrived, I suggest you develop new leaders and share what you have learned, or at least write a book so we all can learn more. I don't plan on ever "arriving." I always want to be learning to see and feel things differently than before. If anyone ever tells you that you ask too many questions, consider finding a new mentor or readjust your approach.

Leaders learn by grasping.

Grasp on to the gold nuggets, the new shiny examples that help propel you forward as a leader. I use the word grasp because I want you to pay the price to never let go of what you have learned. If it costs you a lot, you will take better care of it. Some of the lessons you observe will seem meaningless or like they are way over your head. Grasp them anyway. Make them yours in the context necessary for your career. Don't let go of them. You may never see them again.

Along these same lines, leaders know they are in for a lifetime of learning. It's a totally different mindset. I look at Jack Welch, the former CEO of GE. After his retirement, he is sharing his leadership values and he is still learning. Learning didn't end with his retirement. I see other leaders who retire and then they go play golf. They do not invest in others and they do not have a desire to keep on learning. They shut themselves off. I guess they were OK for the time they were in the game, but now they have sadly become dinosaurs. I can't help wondering why they decided to stop learning or investing in others. Don't let that be you. You can never learn enough. You can never invest enough in others. You can never be too effective. I had a man in my nursing class in college who was 50. He ended one career only to start another. I had a retired pharmacist in his 80's in my meteorology class. He still wanted to learn more. I look back with so much admiration for those two men. They didn't allow others to influence them to stop learning. They went after their lifetime of learning. I have met 80 year olds who were more like 50 years old in their mind sets. There bodies weren't reacting like they used to, but their minds were strong and vibrant. You are never too old to learn. Stay sharp mentally and professionally by developing yourself and developing others.

Chapter 2
LEADERSHIP IS IMPARTED

"The true aim of everyone who aspires to be a teacher should be, not to impart his own opinions, but to kindle minds."
—Frederick William Robertson

Leadership is not only learned it is imparted. Much of it is learned through an impartation process. In life, it is said that only true change comes through In life, it is said that only true change comes through a significant event. That could said be in the development of a leader as well. A significant event doesn't have to be a tragic or even a bad event. It just has to be an event that alters how one performs and perceives things. The one who has the value imparted to them has to use their minds and allow the impartation to take a deep root in their life. A leader who has had leadership tools imparted to them and then develops the associated characteristics will be successful.

As a young leader, I thought like a young leader. Now, as a seasoned leader, I think like a seasoned leader should. Years ago, before certain events or occurrences changed my life I would have acted out of a certain degree of immaturity. Since I have had certain leadership characteristics imparted to me, I now respond instead of reacting. Notice the difference. One is a choice and one is reflex.

Like many of the other lessons I write about, impartation is an active participative event. In other words, you do it on purpose. You do it with a purpose, and for a purpose. You are calculating your career and growth and you understand what it takes to become who it is you desire to become.

Leadership is all about the people. You will see that theme throughout almost all the books and presentations I give. I don't expect everyone to take my statements at face value. However, this life has to be about more than the bottom line on a financial statement. You don't lead a bottom line. People produce that bottom line. I have written before and I stand by my statements that if I take care of my people they will in turn take care of the rest. In the December 2005 issue of Business 2.0 Magazine, David Neeleman founder, chairman, and CEO of Jet Blue stated that he had learned so much by observing his grandfather who ran a general store. Neeleman, in speaking of his grandfather said, "He never told me, "take care of others, and they'll take care of you." He didn't have to. I saw it happen." He went on to say that when he entered the airline industry he, "never thought in terms of passengers or tickets sold," but of "customers" and passengers." My reason for bringing this up was that his grandfather imparted this service value of people to his grandson, who in turn did his part in learning by observing and then placing integrity to the value by living it by example in his leadership lessons. It's the same with me as a leader, if I provide them a good atmosphere complete with leadership, imparting vision, and goals, and actually caring about them, then they will take care of the rest. Mr. Neeleman said he didn't have to be verbally told that lesson. Now, before you get too critical of me, I need to clarify something. No matter how well I lead people and care for them I still have someone who is always trying to prove me wrong. I can take care of my employees in a grand manner and still have someone taking it easy and not helping our team be the best it can be. My philosophy, that I just shared, actually works about 80-90 percent of the time. The 10-20 percent of the time when it doesn't work, I end up in my office engaged in long discussions where I do most of the talking to the offender.

It doesn't matter whether or not there are distractions; it is still about imparting to the people. I have heard it said, and I do believe that people don't care how much I know as a leader, until they know how much I care about them. Read that again. Think about it and see if you are that way. I find that if I don't believe someone actually cares about me, I limit my time with them. I also find that people tend to disengage when they think the person talking to them doesn't actually care about them. I know I do. They listen to words spoken but they filter them without commitment. People, your people, need to know you care. When that happens the door to being able to impart to them will swing wide open.

I like what Tom Landry once said. When he was asked about his ability to lead, he said the following, "I get people to do the things they don't want to do in order to get the things they want." In other words, he motivated people to pay the price and do the hard work in order to win the championships they desired. One thing I noticed in this as well was that they may not win the championship, but his teams always put themselves in a place to compete for the championship. That's imparting leadership.

I want to stress something else in the imparting process. Carefully think about this next statement. IT'S NOT ABOUT THE LEADER! That's correct. It's not about us as leaders. It is about whom we lead. Leaders learn to love their people. I have made that statement several times and watched peoples eyes roll back in their head. Think about love. Love is a commitment. It isn't a feeling. If leaders always lead people by how they feel, failure would surely follow. I never lead by how I feel. I leave my feelings at the door. For instance, if I am angry, often times my teams will never know it. That's not being fake. I shouldn't be placing my shortcomings on my teams. My teams don't need to look over their shoulders wondering if their job is on the line or why their leader is in a bad mood. They shouldn't have to bear that burden and have to concentrate on their job at the same time. A leader who allows themself to walk around in a bad mood thinks that everything is about them and how they feel. It is not. It's about the team, our team, the people. Sure, I make mistakes and sometimes my anger or other mood may show. We are all human and we all at times exhibit our humanness. Let's let the bad exhibits be few and far between until they are nearly nonexistent. Don't allow them to lessen your fruitfulness as a leader.

Learn to love in a healthy manner. Learn to show your people you care. They may surprise you when you realize what they are really capable of accomplishing.

Chapter 3
LEADERS HAVE A VISION

"True Originality consists not in a new manner but in a new vision."
—*Edith Wharton*

I can hear the groans of the masses. There are so many overused words and under realized dreams. I am not talking in this chapter about being a visionary. Being a visionary and having a vision isn't necessarily the same thing. Having a vision means you know the direction you want to go and you see the result you desire long before it is manifested. You can see the end before it is ever manifested in reality. You may not know all the nuts and bolts of everything. You don't have to. Having a vision allows a company and a team to move in a direction knowing what end result you desire. For instance, a high school student has a vision to achieve a college degree. The student rarely knows what they want the degree in; however, they know they want a college degree. They have the vision for the degree, even though they can't see exactly what the end result will be. The end result unfolds as they move in the direction of the vision. It's the vision that keeps them moving forward so that it all plays out and they achieve their desired result.

In healthcare, I often strive to impart a vision of cost, service, and quality. Our customers know what they want. They want controlled reasonable costs, good timely customer service, and a quality of care that restores their health. That vision was imparted to me early on by other healthcare leaders.

The challenge of a leader is to get the employees to buy into that vision, understand it, and put processes in place that enhance and complete that vision. You have the vision. Now get the tools in place to inspire and lead your people who will complete that vision.

My personal opinion is one in which people are the end result. No matter what business you are in, it's all about people. People will make the product, service, and quality that other people will buy and use. It's all about the people. Invest in the people.

Leaders know who imparts the vision. They do. That is the leader's responsibility. They can dissect the vision and know the vision inside and out. That allows the leader to be able to put in place the tools necessary for imparting the vision. The tools are often different for the visions being imparted. You must be alert to what is necessary to impart the vision. The tools are as varied as the people carrying out the vision.

Leaders also know who carries out the vision. If the leader imparts the vision correctly, the people will carry it out and fulfill it correctly. As a consultant, I often ask divisions of institutions to tell me the direction they are heading. I will ask them questions such as, "Do you know where you are going as a group?" I have never received a good answer. Most of the time, I never get an answer. I get more looks of disappointment or embarrassment than anything else. I let them know it isn't their problem. It is because of a lack of leadership that they are in the position they are. I often shake my head at how leadership can allow institutions to not have a vision of where they are going. More so, I am appalled at how the leadership doesn't at least communicate it better than they do. The vision is more than just the bottom line of finances. Sure, we all know that if we don't have good finances we won't be in business very long. That's not rocket science. Nevertheless, how do you expect a good bottom line without investing properly in your people? The people, not the leader will carry out the vision. As an example, I don't see the President out fighting the war on the street. I don't see the Generals fighting hand to hand or tank combat. I find the aforementioned imparting the vision and giving those who carry out the vision the tools to be successful. That doesn't lessen the value of the leader; it strengthens it. We would be wise as leaders to do the same.

I want to add one last thing. A good leader will get out of the way of the people in order to carry out the vision. They will not allow themselves to be an obstacle or to impede the progress of success. Good leaders impart the vision, they give their people the tools to be successful, and then they hold them accountable for the end result. You can't hold someone accountable who hasn't been given the tools and responsibility to be successful. A leader cannot ask their team to be successful with one arm tied behind their back. They can't be held accountable or responsible for anything they haven't been given the tools and authority to change. Getting out of the way doesn't mean total hands off. You have to have a presence and allow your people to see that you are in the battles of life with them and that you know and understand what they are going through. People often times don't care if you as a leader don't have all the answers. They do want to see that you understand what they are going through and can show some empathy and compassion.

As a leader impart the vision, give the tools necessary to make your team successful, and then get out of the way. You may be surprised at how well your teams do.

Chapter 4
LEADERS HAVE A PRESENCE

"The best effect of fine persons is felt after we have left their presence." —Ralph Waldo Emerson

Leaders have a presence. I am going to discuss having a presence in several different terms. First, let us discuss the presence or aura that a true leader possesses. Hollywood calls it star power. I don't like that term. I am talking about the presence one possesses that when they walk into a room people take notice. They carry themselves with a confidence in the direction they are going and the vision they are carrying. This isn't arrogance. It is confidence. It isn't a false confidence; it is a natural ability they have developed over time. They may be nervous about meeting payroll and they may be nervous about other things but you can't tell it by how they carry themselves and the presence they exude.

The other presence I want to discuss is what I mentioned in an earlier chapter. A leader has a presence amongst their staff. I cannot emphasize enough how important this is. You can't change a culture without being involved in it. You can't be involved in it by being absent from it. A leader has to see and experience for themself the inner workings of the culture of their organization in order to truly understand what needs to change. I have seen so many CEOs who consider themselves leaders who really aren't. They are in positions of leadership, but they work more like a CFO or COO than a CEO does. They are interested in and work the finances but have little contact with their people. They hire people to run different aspects of the organization and they hold those people accountable. Then they fire them based upon others input after things have gotten so bad they have to make a change or risk being fired themselves.

If things have gotten that bad, what do you think the reasons are? I believe it is usually related in part to the leader not having a presence in their place of business. I do go to other businesses and see the CEO eating lunch with the people and joking with the people and getting a sense of the atmosphere of the culture. That is a true leader. They lead by example and aren't afraid to have a presence amongst their team. I am appalled when I see people in positions of leadership who shouldn't be there. They have a false concept of who they really are. They aren't afraid to use their authority. It's actually sad they have to use their authority. That's usually because no one respects them.

It is one thing to be in authority, it is another thing to have to use it. A leader doesn't wield their authority like a sword. Authority is only necessary when you need to use it in a healthy manner to get a job done. I have seen it used when it was the last resort and it never should have had to be used that way.

Leaders develop and accept personal accountability. Excuses embarrass leaders. I never offer excuses. I rarely offer reasons during hard times. I look to lead for the end result. Everything that happens under my responsibility, I have to answer for as a leader. The leaders to whom I am accountable aren't interested in excuses. I am not either. Therefore, I rarely, if ever, make time to give an excuse.

I often tell people I am coaching to, "not be an excuse looking for a place to happen." I encourage them to be engaged and develop an understanding of how things work the way they do and to proactively head off any potential problems they may have coming toward them. It is better that way than to act like a victim of circumstance or lack of vision.

Chapter 5
LEADERS DEVELOP INTANGIBLES

*"The positive thinker sees the invisible,
feels the intangible, and achieves the impossible."*
—*Anonymous*

Leaders have certain characteristics that are not always identifiable, even when you see them in action. I call those characteristics, "intangibles." The dictionary defines intangible as something that cannot be defined by the senses. Characteristics such as goodwill or dedication are two such intangibles. You can see a leader exhibit those characteristics, but you can't hold them in your hand. I hear sports announcers using the words with liberty as well when they speak of a player being teachable. They are characteristics not seen with the naked eye but perceived by the senses. They are perceived; they are not defined by the senses.

I often hear people say, "He or she has IT." What is IT? I find that IT is the intangible that makes you hire someone for the very purpose you need and at the right time. Sometimes "IT" is only needed for a season, not forever. Sometimes "IT" is needed forever.

I am sure you can name some intangibles of your own. Perhaps confidence, calm, cool, and collected. When you see someone who has intangibles you find yourself attracted to them. You sense you are attracted for all the right reasons. That is healthy.

One intangible I find that a leader must possess is temperament. Temperament at times has a negative connotation. What I want to do is give you the positive connotation. Temperament is the manner of thinking and behaving in an acceptable way that the current position you are in demands you be. That temperament is establishing a new culture.

I have found leaders who enter into a job or position with what seems to be the right temperament, but who seem to lose it at the wrong time. Temperament is a characteristic that must be monitored. A leader cannot turn it off and on. You have to have it to be successful. When a leader is losing the temperament necessary for the job they are doing, they either take a rest and recharge their batteries or they need to move on. Those are two extremes. However, I do not believe there is a true middle ground. I find when one hangs on, it is like a slow amputation. It is very painful until it is cut off. It is very painful for both parties involved. Never underestimate temperament. Develop it, nurture it, and by all means let it be a part of your intangibles.

Another intangible is attitude. Have you ever tried to identify an attitude? You see someone with a bad attitude and then they smile and tell you they don't have an attitude. They hide it. You cannot hold the attitude in your hand. It isn't a physical characteristic although it has more of a spiritual substance to it. You confront someone on their attitude only to be told they really don't have one. You cannot take it out and show it to them. Nevertheless, take heed you can still confront it. How you ask? Every attitude manifests itself in some way. Bad attitudes are manifested in anger, and in sarcasm. Those manifestations I have mentioned are what you use to confront the attitude. You can show them when they were angry or acting out and hand them the end result. As a leader, you can't have a bad attitude. It will cost you your career. Hopefully, by the time you are in position you will have dealt with any attitudes that may cost you.

Let me summarize attitude by saying that attitude is baggage better left at the door. A leader definitely cannot afford to be seen with an attitude that is negative. Always guard and protect your career with temperament.

Chapter 6
LEADERS WORK THEMSELVES OUT OF A JOB

*"One machine can do the work of 50 ordinary men.
No machine can do the work of one extraordinary man."*
—Elbert Hubbard

I can hear everyone saying whoa, whoa, put the breaks on there, Sparky! Just give me a moment to explain what I mean. This is a good thing. Leaders who effectively do their job make it such that their people are functioning in the manner expected, and working efficiently, without the leader's physical presence among them. The culture has become one in which the only acceptable way of acting has become the one the leader has set by example. I have heard it said that people use the "culture" as an excuse. Whether they do or not isn't the issue. Every organization has a defined culture. You can't get around it. It may be negative and self-defeating, or it may be one of superior customer service, but it is still a culture. I like cultures where leaders empower their employees.

Leaders let those who need to do their thing, do it, and then they get out of the way. The leader doesn't want to mess it up. It isn't a pride thing that needs recognition. It is a pride thing in that the leader invests themself in such a way that they are proud that the end result was realized. It's a pride that has a foundation of humility with it. It's not a false pride or a recognition thing that leaders need. Because, after all, it was an investment in the people that the leader desired and achieved. Very simply put, the leader has positively worked themself out of a job and can now move on to the next calling and vision they receive.

Chapter 7
LEADERS EXHIBIT SELF-CONTROL

*"Self discipline is that which, next to virtue,
truly and essentially raises one man above another."*
—Joseph Addison

Self-control is a fruit of the spirit that is missing in so many people in today's world. I find it interesting how we as leaders can lead such large or small organizations and lack self control in areas so vital to our character and life. Self-control is not an option. It is not a Self-control is not an option. It is not a switch to be turned on or off. It is necessary for living and working within the established boundaries one has to have to protect all that is vital to them. With self-control, emotions are disciplined, finances are secured, health is restored and maintained, and relationships are protected. With self-control, you can attain nearly everything you desire as a leader. Have you witnessed what happens when leaders don't exhibit self-control? Do I need to mention recent Presidential behaviors? How about corporate executives going to jail? These things did not have to happen. Greed often times overrides our character when we allow self-control to go unchecked. When we ignore self-control we allow fleshly or carnal desires to override common sense.

I have noticed that leaders who exhibit self-control don't draw attention to themselves but to the end result. They realize it isn't all about them. It is about the discipline that enhances self-control. They let their Yes be Yes and their No be No. There isn't any wavering and inconsistency. They aren't soft minded. They have made up their minds and set their will to be constant. You can count on these types of leaders because you know what to expect and what you will get. There is a certain amount of security involved in that. People like security and a certain amount of control.

One way I see self-control exhibited is in the way a leader dresses. Yes, I am speaking of the way they wear their clothes and what clothes they wear. I read a book called, "Roger's Rules for Success." In that book he wrote, "Never let your dress be second guessed." I read that book nearly twenty years ago and it stuck with me. I wear dress suits to work and some people can't figure out why I would always wear a suit. I will always be accused of being overdressed, never underdressed. It doesn't bother me when I am criticized by someone for being overdressed. That's because I set my own standard in dress; I don't follow anyone else. It also amazes me when someone has the gall to mention someone's dress. To me, clothes and style are personal. I don't mention to others anything about their attire unless it is about a coworker being inappropriately dressed. Otherwise, it's none of my business. In today's world, it is chic to dress down such as in the research and development world, and computer sciences industry. As a leader, I am after more than just how a person dresses. That is an individual quality. Most of these things happen because a leader tries to be everything to everybody. As a leader, your responsibility is to be stable and consistent. Don't place yourself in a position or institution where everything is second-guessed. Be a leader in everything you do.

Chapter 8
LEADERS SEE AND HEAR THINGS

"A wise man can see more from the bottom of a well than a fool can from a mountain top." —Unknown

Leaders see and hear things. I am not talking about schizophrenia, of which many a leader may be accused. Any leader, who has a vision, has one accused. Any leader, who has a vision, has one because of what they see and hear. Leaders have many voices talking to them and pulling at them. It is the voice they give attention to that will determine their direction, and the difference between success and failure.

What do you see? Can you see it materialize before you have a finished product in your hand? Most architects and artists have this ability. I also believe any leader who has a vision that they can't rest from until it is accomplished, can do the same. One more thing, it's just as important to realize that what you don't see can harm you as well.

I am a former trauma nurse. I worked for years as a nurse in victims came to us for care was that it wasn't what we saw that bothered us, but rather what we didn't see. We could see a low blood pressure measurement; however, we couldn't see what was causing it. That usually took a surgeon opening them up and surgically repairing whatever was causing them to bleed internally. We couldn't physically see it with our eyes, yet we knew it was happening and there would be a bad result if we didn't act quickly. The same can be said of us as leaders. Without having our fingers on the pulse of the organization, it could cost us our professional lives. We have all seen many an organization fail because of this. Be aware and be just. Don't let what you don't see be the very thing that defeats you as a leader and an organization.

What do you hear? Is it the song you heard on the radio as you drove to work or is it the sound of success as you prepared yourself to win? As leader, you have to listen to voices that pull you toward your goals. I most certainly recommend that if other voices are pulling at you, you make every effort to silence them. I am hoping you have common sense when reading this. I am not suggesting we close out the voices of our families or children or loved ones and our sense of responsibility to the world and nation as a whole. I am suggesting that if you have voices pulling at you to overeat while you are dieting—you silence those voices. You silence the voice of the accusers who accuse you of being blind and selfish or not having the best interest of the corporation at heart. Tune out the voices of self-doubt and self-deprecation. Tune in the voices that direct, give guidance and propel you toward success. Even the smallest of steps will make you a winner.

If you cannot see it, or you cannot hear it, you cannot have it.

Chapter 9
LEADERS HAVE FOLLOWERS

" A great Leader never sets himself above his followers except in carrying responsibilities."
—Jules Ormont

Every leaders has followers. If a leader doesn't have followers or people who have doesn't have followers or people who have bought into their vision, then they probably aren't leaders in the true sense of the word. Leaders know that to be successful with their followers they themselves also have to be followers. If one doesn't know how to follow then one certainly does not know how to lead. The two concepts co-exist. I remind people that following is not a weakness. Following is a choice. Every NFL quarterback follows his head coach. Every teacher follows the principle that follows the directions of the superintendent. There is a hierarchy in life whether we like it or not. That doesn't constitute weakness. Rather, it infers order. All leaders have to have order within their organizations no matter how big or small.

Leaders give respect to followers. Followers aren't simpletons. They are human beings who have dreams and families and goals of their own. I suggest that as good leaders you always remember that and never forget it in your dealings with your people.

Leaders extend mercy to all their followers and coworkers. After all, they are the ones carrying out the vision the leader has set forth. If you, as a leader, aren't perfect, don't expect your coworkers or followers to be any different. We are all human. It's OK. We are all fallible. That's OK too. Just extend mercy and you will be given mercy as well. One thing I want to add about extending mercy. Learn this next statement. Leaders do not allow others to confuse being nice with being weak.

Being nice and appropriate is not being weak. I have known leaders who walk around like bullies. You know the type. Not only are they not smiling, but they are wearing a scowl on their face. They use intimidation as a management tool. What fools! As I mentioned earlier intimidation is not a tool to be used. I know some will disagree with this but think of this for a second. If you have to walk around acting tough and wearing a scowl on your face, what does that say about the culture of your organization and your leadership abilities? Organizations should not live by the rule that says, "If Daddy isn't happy then no one is happy." That means that you have created an organization that revolves around the leader and not around the vision. I don't want to work in that organization. You can walk softly and carry a big stick. As leaders, though, make sure the stick is a tool to help others.

One last thing I would like to add to this chapter. A good leader allows themself to be vulnerable. A leader understands that being vulnerable isn't a weakness; it is a character trait. One can walk in a manner where their employees feel they are approachable. As a leader, you don't have to have all the answers all the time. I relieved myself of feeling that way a long time ago. It isn't a weakness to not have all the answers. It is a weakness to not go after and discover the answers. Even though a leader practices being vulnerable, they don't allow themself to become too casual with their employees. The reason is that being casual can diminish a leader's effectiveness. Being vulnerable is a trait I wish to see more leaders exhibit.

Chapter 10
LEADERS ARE SERVANTS

"We teachers can only help the work going on, as servants wait upon the master." —Maria Montessori

Being a servant has taken on such a ban meaning. Our society is one in which everyone is fighting for their rights and believes that being a servant is equal to being a slave. As I wrote in my book, Excel At Living A Centered Life, being a servant is a choice, being a slave isn't a choice. One is freedom the other is bondage. I am a servant to my coworkers, my spouse, my children, and this society. I ask what can I do for my people, not what can they do for me. A person who serves always has a position among their peers. People cannot live without people who serve. Having a service attitude isn't weak and demeaning. It is a choice. The value is layered in their lives like an onion, one layer at a time.

Leaders who serve know they don't deserve to be leaders; they earn their way into leadership through attitude and action. I have seen many people who think that they are better than anyone else is, therefore they should be "made" the leader. I don't think so. That person needs to learn some perspective. At the very least, that person needs to be around people of higher caliber than they are so that they can not only learn a little humility, but also to bring their own level up a few notches.

Leaders make themselves leaders and are called. They are called and chosen or appointed. They are not self-anointed. They may prepare themselves but they aren't self righteous about it. They know there is no room for arrogance. They also know they are there to serve and they aren't ashamed of it. Count me in that group.

Chapter 11
LEADERS MAKE THOSE AROUND THEM BETTER

"It is a common delusion that you make things better by talking about them." —Dame Rose Macaulay

As a young leader, I knew this concept was crucial. If I have a leader who makes me better, then I am destined for success. To make one better one has to embrace the disciplines the leaders may set forth. Just hanging around, or watching the leader, or being a part of the management team will not be enough. You, as a leader, will have to embrace what it takes to get better. This isn't always easy.

As a young nurse, I would work for NFL players and as a trainer at their football camps. I would treat injuries for them. I would always listen to them talk about the coach and the high level of demands he would place on them. However, most all of them embraced what the coach demanded, because they knew how long and tough the road was that lay before them.

As a leader, you should create an atmosphere that at the very least would allow your employees the opportunity to get better. I don't believe that you as the leader have to make them better. Being around you and watching your influence and affluence should make them want to be better. You, as a leader, cannot control anyone, therefore, you as a leader, cannot change anyone. Likewise, no one can change you either. As a leader, you can influence someone to want to be better. Most of the time, your colleagues are looking to be better. That being the case, lead them to ways to be better. Help them raise their levels of expectations so that they can reap better rewards. A leader raises the level of professionalism and service by raising the level of expectations.

You raise the level of expectations by raising the level of thinking. One has to develop new mindsets in order to change. You, as a leader, cannot remain the same by embracing the same old mindsets. You cannot build a spacecraft by looking at the plans of how to build a lawnmower. You cannot build a new company and lead it into the 21st century by building it with the plans that made a company successful in the 19th century. There are some foundational elements, such as building your company on good customer services, competitive pricing, and delivering high quality, that will always under gird your business. However, the markets are different now, the needs are different now, and the resources are different now. Consequently, that means that we, as leaders, have to be different now.

One last note: Just because the world is changing and places high demands on you as a leader, do not fear. Rise to the occasion.

Chapter 12
LEADERS HOLD THEMSELVES ACCOUNTABLE

"To succeed as a team is to hold all of the members accountable for their expertise." —Mitchell Caplan

How many business have we witnessed go bankrupt because they couldn't hold themselves accountable. hey mishandled funds, employees, their futures, and then made their way into bankruptcy and foreclosure. Where were those who should have been holding the leaders accountable? Why didn't the leaders hold themselves accountable? Why did they allow greed to blind them? Did they really believe they wouldn't be held accountable in the end? Didn't the fear of being locked in a prison and losing their reputations cause them to rethink anything? Obviously, it did not. I find my heart breaking as a leader to witness the futures of such great leaders going down in flames of unnecessary complacency and self-centeredness. I grieve for their families and the reputations they have lost because of what someone else did to them. Holding yourself accountable to the employees and the board is a noble thing. It isn't being handcuffed in bondage; rather, it is being freed to move with the guidelines of success. Accountability allows a foundation of success to be stable. As a leader never underestimate the foundation that needs to be laid in order for you to enjoy long-term successes.

I find it amusing that a leader would ever allow themself to think it is a weakness to be held accountable. Being held accountable should instill a good sense of fear and respect for one's responsibilities and to whom a leader is ultimately responsible.

Don't allow anyone to convince you otherwise. Many careers have been brought to a new low because of no accountability. It will catch up with you. It is just a matter of when and where. This is a sobering message. Be accountable and teach accountability.

Chapter 13
LEADERS GIVE PERMISSION

"It is easier to get forgiveness than permission."
—*Stuart's Law of Retroaction*

Giving permission and seeking permission are noble actions. I can see leaders in their arrogance that might be thinking they will never ask for permission for anything. To them I suggest they go back and read the previous chapter. A leader assumes risks. Part of risk taking is allowing your people to be all they need to be. A leader gives themself and their people permission to succeed. I have said this in many conferences only to watch the attendees' eyes roll in disgust. They look at me like, "no kidding." However, how many of us have actually verbally told our teams that they have permission to be successful? I guarantee you that most leaders have given their people the tools to be successful, but rarely inspired them to be successful. Most of the time, it's because leaders automatically think that their teams automatically think success. This simply isn't true. As I consult with many organizations, I find that the people on the foundational levels rarely believe they are a success. They may understand what they do. They understand they are held accountable for cleaning floors, selling a product, or whatever. But when I have been called into a business to turn things around I find that most of the time the people feel they can't do anything without first running it by the leader. Now, if I am a successful leader, why in the world would I ever want them to run everything by me? That is not giving them permission to be successful. It is giving them permission to ask me for permission. That's different from giving them permission to be successful. It is telling them that only I know what will make them successful. I am not asking for agreement with anyone reading this. I am writing this because I witness it everywhere I go.

Leaders, give yourself and your people permission to be successful by not babysitting everything they do. They are educated and quite capable of doing their jobs. Allow them to do their job so that you can then go and prepare the company for the future and not have your hands unnecessarily in the present. As a leader, you can have your hands "on the present," which is different than "in the present." Having your hands on the present allows you to maintain perspective on the current status. Having your hands in the present prevents you from moving forward at the pace necessary for the future of your organization and is usually called micromanagement.

Another equally important rule is giving yourself and your people permission to fail. What? Fail? Are you crazy? Bear with me for a second. As I mentioned earlier, when I go into a business and consult I find people who are afraid to do anything without permission. Then, when I give them a task or project I find them afraid to move forward for fear of failure. I reassure my teams that I encourage them to try even if they fail. It's OK! I found I couldn't get my teams off the starting line so to speak, because they were fearful of what I might do as a leader if they failed. I might add, I inherited these cultures—I didn't establish them. I have some pretty funny stories I share when I speak to groups and conference attendees about these times. I will save those for another time though.

Failure is just a moment in time. Failure does not define you anymore than success defines you. I am more than my successes and I am more than my failures. I have had my share of both. Any leader who tries new things will also have their fair share as well. It's OK! Don't let failures define you and don't let it define your employees or organization either. I will give you one simple example. Look at the airline industry. That industry has had its share of successes and failures. Yet, we still fly in record numbers. We haven't allowed those failures or successes to define that industry. We, as consumers, have determined that the successes and failures of the airline industry are inherent risks with the industry itself. If we allow that for the airline industry, then why don't we allow it for our industries as well? Give your people permission to fail; they may surprise you with twice as much success.

I mentioned earlier in the chapter that part of being a leader is taking risks. I stand by that. Take the risk of allowing your employees the boundaries to succeed and to fail. Risk isn't a dirty word. It is a verb. It is an action. As a leader, you don't sit idly by and take risk. You actively engage yourself in risk taking. It can be healthy. I have never seen anyone have success without risk. Be an active risk taker, not fearing failure, and impart that to your team and organization. I coached little league baseball and basketball. I had kids tell me they wouldn't swing the bat because they were afraid they would strike out. Guess what? They struck out whether they swung the bat or not. I encouraged them to risk it. Occasionally, even my worst player hit the ball just because he swung the bat. I had kids who wouldn't shoot the basketball because they were afraid they would miss. I actually think they were afraid of what people would think of them if they missed. I encouraged them to shoot anyway, that we had people to get the rebound if they missed.

In all earnest I think our organizations can be like that. I encourage my employees to go for it, swing away, shoot for glory! At least we went for it and probably learned something along the way!

Chapter 14
LEADERS WORK TO BECOME LEADERS

"The longer I live the more beautiful life becomes."
—*Frank Lloyd Wright*

It is a known fact that leaders work to become the leader they desire to be. They grasp at the opportunities available to become more proficient in all facets of their management and leadership skill development. Leaders understand that their level of influence is as strong as their ability to keep building and girding up the foundation of skills. Leaders know it often takes time to develop. They aren't made proficient overnight. They develop basic skills such as learning to plan, organize, and monitor progress without others looking over their shoulders. They are self-motivated to a point that they desire their own progress even when no one else is watching. Then, as they are placed in the environment as a leader, they continue to develop the necessary communication and observation skills that help them maximize employee and business development. These skills are necessary to ensure your success in any environment that is rapidly changing due to market volatility, competition, and customer demands.

During this time of development, the leader learns what roles and expectations are being placed upon them by everyone from external to internal customers, and their bosses or leaders. You learn through observing supervisory styles which ones to use and when to use them. You learn which ones are effective and how to make a switch midstream when the situation demands it. Most of this is done by listening and communicating.

    A good leader knows that everything they do and say is being scrutinized by someone, somewhere. They are never "off the record." They have a camera on them full time and are aware that someone is always watching. Therefore, the foundational tools such as time management, speech control, dress, communication, and listening skills, are all developed to a high level of quality in the life of the leader. They are critical to sustaining the career of the leader.

Chapter 15
LEADERS CREATE HIGH QUALITY ENVIRONMENTS

"It is quality rather than quantity that matters."
—*Seneca*

Creating a high quality environment is creating a lasting environment. Environments are living breathing entities that are made up of intelligently functioning members. Being involved in a high quality environment demands your presence as a leader and your input, as you give direction to the acceptable and unacceptable norms. In this process, leaders learn to govern and lead by giving and receiving constructive criticism in a healthy manner. They learn to minimize any defensiveness and head it off before it happens. They take into consideration the feelings of others and the effect their criticism may have on the individuals concerned. This is crucial in the fact that it can taint and set forth an unhealthy environment if workers are in a bad mood all day. The consideration of how criticisms will be received should not change the fact that it must be done. It should, however, alter any way the leader may unknowingly be stepping on a landmine. During this process, the leader can assess their coaching and communication strengths and identify opportunities for improvement. They can use their coaching to improve the environment and get the results they are looking for.

After all, a leader is looking to create a highly motivated environment. Not everyone hears criticism the same nor do they always know what to do with it. It's no different for the leader either. Just as in life, leadership has to be learned to be handled intelligently. That means the leader uses fluid thought processes to develop a clear mind, thereby making the way for intelligent, well thought out, outcomes. I have seen the most intelligent people make the dumbest errors in calculations. Leaders learn to temper discipline with intelligence. Use the necessary tools at your disposal to maximize the performance you desire and achieve the environment you are working so hard to achieve.

Chapter 16
LEADERS LOOK TO IMPROVE THEIR EFFECTIVENESS

"People, like nails, lose their effectiveness when they lose direction and begin to bend."
—Walter Savage Landor

Leaders are always looking to improve their effectiveness. I have met many people in leadership positions who believe that they have already surpassed all the knowledge they could ever need. I have met very few who I believe actually have surpassed it all. As I mentioned earlier in the book, leadership requires a lifetime of learning. You need to be actively acquiring the skills necessary in order to meet the challenges that lie ahead. These skills will serve you well as you are faced with challenges you never dreamed you would be met with. These challenges can have either a positive or a negative effect on you depending on how thoroughly you prepared yourself to confront them.

Leaders often find that not only are they acquiring skills to meet their own challenges, they are often times realizing that the focus isn't just on them. A true leader is always interested in employee development and meeting the needs of all the team members. Cultures are more diverse today than ever. One size doesn't fit all. You have to anticipate needs and create a culture where the members can trust and expect that you will be consistent and lead the way in meeting their needs. Remember, earlier I wrote that no one cares how much you know, until they know how much you care.

In caring, you will have to develop relationships that will serve as the structure of your environment. You will be using thinking and speaking skills, relating skills, directing skills, and definitely listening skills. Don't be fooled, even when one is listening, one is communicating. There will be many times you will need to move from being the boss to being a coach, and perhaps a friend, within certain trusted and established rules. Keep on determining ways to motivate people and understand their values. Reward them with the positive feedback. Never let any positive feedback be fake or not heartfelt. That will be smelled like a rat a mile away and it will ultimately cause mistrust, as members will think you are just self-serving. You will need to develop skills to overcome any resistance and then maximize those skills to break through the hard times.

Know that what is important to you isn't always important to your employees. You have to get people interested in what is important to you by showing them the effect it will have on their outcomes or current environment. If it doesn't affect them, chances are it won't mean anything to them, and they will tend to dismiss it.

As a leader always look to improve your effectiveness by monitoring your progress based upon the results you are seeing manifested through the members of your environment and culture. Make changes where necessary and fine tune to keep it moving forward without fail. Your effectiveness will be determined by your colleagues' outcomes.

Chapter 17
LEADERS PERFORM SELF ASSESSMENT

"I never saw an ugly thing in my life: for let the form of an object be what it may—light, shade, perspective will always make it beautiful." —John Constable

You will read several times throughout this book. One of those themes is self assessment. I believe that great leaders are constantly involved in assessing and reassessing their skills and actions. This isn't second-guessing. It is a process of evaluating your talents and skills and the best use that you are making of them. Many people will benefit from you going through these actions. You will be identifying what you do well and what you need to improve upon.

As you assess, strive to understand the difference between your responsibilities and those of your staff. A personal example I will share is one that I find happens in healthcare. In smaller hospitals staffing is a major issue. Often times the director or manager of the unit will perform clinical duties along with their managerial duties. I find, though, that when a manager performs one the other tends to suffer. I worked in one facility as an interim director to help re-establish them as a viable entity. The people were used to having their Director in scrubs and not wearing a tie. They had seven different directors in 10 years and three in the last five. They asked me why I wasn't wearing scrubs and working in the clinical area. I asked them how well it worked for them when the previous managers were in scrubs and working clinically. It didn't. The place was missing even the basic foundations expected from any regulatory agency. I taught them my responsibilities compared to theirs. There was no way I would have been successful doing what they thought I should be doing. It all worked out fine and equilibrium was restored.

I did this by improving communication and setting up mutual expectations. The staff knew what was expected of them and they knew what they could expect of me. I didn't do this with an in your face type of attitude toward them. I did it by educating them and adapting my leadership style in the manner that was necessary to meet the standards of where we needed to go.

I have to admit; at times not everyone will be on board with your ideas. You will have those who are engaged and those taking a wait and see approach. To those waiting to see, I had a conversation with them to influence them to get on board or off. I didn't do it in a harsh way. I explained that I needed them and their colleagues needed them as well. There isn't any place safe for bystanders and Monday morning quarterbacks in the leadership world I am in. As I coached and led through having a presence, we were able to move forward and I noticed staff morale and performance improving. Staff members became more engaged and they started going the extra mile when it was needed. Together, we all created a culture we could both work within and be proud. There was nothing easy about it. Then again, if it was easy, why would they need us as leaders?

Chapter 18
LEADERS LEAD PEOPLE AND MANAGE SITUATIONS

"Management is doing things right; Leadership is doing the right things." —Peter Drucker

I once interviewed for a position in an organization where the person I would have reported to stated that he didn't think he could control me. My response was, why would he want to? People aren't to be controlled, they are to be led. If you have the need to control people, go work in a daycare facility. If you want to build a high-powered team, work in a place where the people desire to be led. Leaders lead people and manage situations. This is more than simple semantics and playing with words. I have plenty of people who like to argue this concept with me. My point is that I can't control anyone. Nor do I want to. I let micromanagers do that. As long as you micromanage you will never develop into a leader. I don't have to have total control. The people I lead don't need to feel smothered.

The ultimate in leadership is being a leader who leads leaders. There is security in knowing that the leaders you are leading are your colleagues who challenge you to be better for them. I believe we manage situations. Yes, people are working the situation, but you aren't controlling them. You are leading them and getting out of the way for them to help manage the situation. Everyone has a role in this. One isn't more important than the other. They are too intertwined to be calculated as the most to least important. In these situations you will have people rise to the occasion as people you can motivate and rely on. More will get done because delegation was effectual. The commitment will be outstanding and the job will be finished effectively. You will witness that your confidence as a leader grows as well as observing the confidence of your people in you growing. As a leader, you will get people to do what they need to do and the specific challenges you may have faced at one time will fall by the wayside. All that is accomplished because you decide to lead, impart, and get out of the way. A leader will also notice during this time that they can more effectively move an organization forward by not having to be involved in every minute detail that can be handled and managed by your employees.

While all of this is happening you see an alignment of the values of the organization and that of the employees who make up the organization. It's exciting and rewarding.

Chapter 19
LEADERS RESPOND WHEN CAUGHT OFF GUARD

"From without, no wonderful effect is wrought within ourselves, unless some interior, responding wonder meets it."
—Hermann Melville

If you are a leader worth any salt at all, you will come face to face with times you are caught off guard. It is hard to always be on top of your "A" game. Many times people purposefully place obstacles in your path to catch you off guard. I have personally witnessed leaders with the deer in the headlights look as they stumbled and bumbled through certain unexpected scenarios. Allow me to let you in on a little secret. When you are caught off guard, you need to respond in a healthy manner. It's all about controlling your emotions and your thoughts.

This is a true discipline. I believe quarterbacks, astronauts, parents, physicians, policeman, the President, and others, just to mention a few, have all had to practice this discipline. If you just allow your mind be run on idle all day, unengaged in practical critical thinking patterns, then why would you ever expect to be successful in a crisis? I am not embarrassed when caught off guard. Embarrassment is just an emotion of pride. If you entertain the embarrassment, then the focus is no longer on the incident, but on you as a person. A true leader doesn't allow that to happen. Yes, I have been embarrassed. I have had to redirect my thoughts. That's why I am sharing these leadership lessons with you. I have experienced all that I am sharing with you today. Now, let's go back to the lesson.

The lesson is that leaders respond when caught off guard. Notice the verb. The verb is an action word. It is respond. It is not react. Reacting brings unstable emotions into a situation that produces unstable results. Have you ever been involved in a situation where the atmosphere of anger and fear was so thick you believed you could cut it with a knife?

I have and I will never forget how uncomfortable the leaders made me feel. I made a point to file it in my mental bank so that when I became a leader I wouldn't allow that to happen to my teams. I have been involved in disasters where trains crashed, we received many injured, but you wouldn't know the atmosphere was any different from any other day. I established an environment of productive calm. The atmosphere was set by the leader. People could look at us and see were prepared to move forward in confidence. We all knew what we had to do and we did it. There is an important message to learn here as well.

As a leader, I realized my body language and facial expressions were always being watched. My body language was sending a message to people whether I wanted it to or not. I purposefully walked around with a smile on my face even when my stomach was churning. A leader realizes that he or she sets the tone of the environment by their body language. Walk in with a smile and see how people respond. Walk in angry and see how they scatter. All because of the tone the leader set.

All of the concepts I have set forth are within the scope and control of the leader. You will be caught off guard. I guarantee it. It's not the fact you are caught off guard that is at issue; it's how you deal with it as a leader that will make you a success or failure.

Chapter 20
LEADERS HAVE A PERSONAL PLAN

"In preparing for battle I have always found that plans are useless, but planning is indispensable."
—Dwight D. Eisenhower

If you haven't figured it out yet, life has a way of happening with or without us. The days and years go by whether we move forward or regress. A true leader leads themselves by creating and having a plan. They have personal and professional plans and most of the time they mesh. Earlier we mentioned having vision. You know you can't have a vision come to fruition without having a plan. A personal plan allows you to move from I hope to I am. You move from wondering how we ever got here to how we are going to move out of here. It moves you to a higher level of personal accountability. Dr Robert Schuller says, "If it's going to be it's up to me!" In other words, it isn't going to happen if you don't do it. Moreover, you can't do it without a plan. John Miller of the QBQ.com speaks of personal account-ability. Look at his website, John challenges people to think differently and to accept personal responsibility.

Your personal and professional plan allows you to develop your success and plan your future in a way that helps you strategically move on the right path. Yes, you may have to alter your course at times, but this can be done successfully no matter what obstacles may fall in your path. Remember, you may stumble but you don't have to stay down. Get up, wipe the dust off, and laugh. Then re-establish the plan.

A plan is worthless unless it is being worked. I like the proverb that says a man may plan his course but God directs his footsteps. It is important to know you are a spiritual as well as a physical being. The Proverbs show us that we may choose healthcare as a career but God will help direct us on our path and plan the places we need to be practicing healthcare. If you are alert, you will often times see that you may end up in places you would not have chosen in the natural life on your own. Nonetheless, you wouldn't trade the experiences for either. There is one last thing I want to add about this.

A plan that you establish must take into consideration other people as well. Plans can be lonely if it all centers on only you. When you include others, you will be amazed at how fast forward you will move. Others like to be involved in your life as a leader. Remember Robert Schuller: "If it's going to be it's up to me!"

Chapter 21
LEADERS SURROUND THEMSELVES WITH STRONG PEOPLE

"The best leader is the one who has the sense to surround himself with outstanding people and self-restraint not to meddle with how they do their jobs." —Author Unknown

I know we often think that the leader is the strongest person on the team. That's not always the case. It is true that the leader may be stronger in some traits and skills, however, that doesn't mean they are the strongest. It means that they are the one in the position of leader. I have found that strength often times is relative to the difficult times a leader goes through. You have heard it said that success is difficult to handle. Have you ever questioned why that is? Let's assume it's true for the sake of my illustration. I believe that people have a hard time handling success because it is easily earned. They didn't have to pay a hard price for it. Some pay a hard price of work effort, but not in the old terms of blood, sweat, and tears. When a leader pays the price in blood, sweat and tears they tend to appreciate the success much more than the times the success came easy. When a leader surrounds themself with stronger people, it enhances the success of which they are in search.

As a leader, I find myself gifted in areas that others aren't as gifted in or have a different gifting. As a leader, I need those people who are gifted in the areas in which I am lacking. I find some leaders too arrogant to admit that others could be stronger than them. It isn't a matter of pride to me. I have no problem enjoying others' gifts and the success their gifting brings. It also relieves me of having to be someone that I simply am not. I can enjoy and express my strengths without worry of being someone I am not.

I surround myself with people who are stronger than me in areas of expertise and who can firm up the foundation of the organization of which I am entrusted. I often find it interesting how there are so many people who have not only not paid the price, they really don't even know their strengths well enough to tell others how they should be doing things.

Smart and secure leaders surround themselves with people who are stronger than they are in order to gain the success they all desire as a team. It is a sign of strength when a leader admits he needs people who are stronger than he is. The President of the United States does this when appointing his cabinet. There is no way any one person can be the expert necessary in all areas of foreign and domestic affairs. Subsequently, it is necessary to appoint those who are experts. Remember, when leading a team and organization, it is necessary to surround yourself with people who are stronger than you in their areas of expertise. As I emphasized in an earlier chapter, become a leader who leads leaders.

Chapter 22
LEADERS KNOW THE RULE IS THERE AREN'T ANY RULES

"There are no rules here—we are trying to accomplish something." —Thomas A. Edison

When you read that lesson, I'm sure you just thought that I have no ethics. I am not talking about breaking all the rules and not having ethics. That attitude will land you without a job, or worse, land you in a jail cell next to a guy named "Tiny." What I am talking about is developing an attitude that you aren't going to be confined to the status quo. Leaders know that as the world changes and the market changes, leadership changes. It is an unwritten, but known rule. Often times, rules confine us and keep us from achieving what we desire. There are men and women who led our nation through some of its hardest times and were called for those times. Likewise, there are new developed leaders who are leading us through what appears to be just as hard of times. Leaders know that in order to gain success they can't think like they used to. To move forward requires setting new rules and standards that meet the challenges of the times we face. It means that the leader knows there aren't any rules with which they need to restrict themself.

I have been in so many organizations that restrict themselves with "rules" that they think or remember hearing somewhere. Even when those rules are now archaic, or no longer apply, or were never truly rules at all, they still feel compelled or obligated to handcuff themselves with them. Rules are generally made as guidelines to work within for the protection of the society they are necessary for. They aren't meant to confine a person or organization from moving forward. When a leader grabs this concept, they soon learn to be able to think outside the boundaries in order to enhance or expand the boundaries. They are no longer willing to be restricted and confined by the rules. Often times as a leader you will ask why are we are doing things the way we are doing things and the answer you often receive will be one of, "Well, that's the way we have always done things." Red flags should instantly fly up and announce that change is now in order. It's time to establish new rules or guidelines to move within. Remember ethics and your reputation as a leader is worth more than a pot of gold. You can always replace a pot of gold. You can't replace your reputation. Knowing that the rules are, "There are no rules," is not a license to be unethical. It is knowing that you are now free to think in new and different ways in order to gain the success you desire. Think wisely on this chapter.

Chapter 23
LEADERS ARE LOYAL

"When you are part of team, you stand up for your teammates. Your loyalty is to them. You protect them through good and bad because they would do the same for you."
—Yogi Berra

A leader cannot expect loyalty if they are not willing to be loyal. When I was a child, many of the Major League baseball teams were made up of players who were local or who lived local year round. The players were a part of the community that they played for. In many of the cities that had teams, you could go out and see the ballplayers at local restaurants and the same places where all the average people frequented. The locals could relate to them. Then came free agency and it was all about the money. It was no longer because the player lived in Boston or New York or Kansas City. When that happened the fans were forced to become loyal to the team uniform, instead of to the people wearing the uniform. The fans found they could no longer relate to the individuals because the players didn't stick around long enough to actually be a part of the community. This wasn't always the rule, but it did happen more often than not. Every year when the season starts, I have to check the rosters to see who is playing in a new city now. There are so many new moves. No one seems loyal unless there is a dollar attached. I find true leaders are of course loyal to themselves but they strive for loyalty, even when others around them don't.

Loyalty is a true character trait. How many of us have heard people say I will be loyal to them as long as they are loyal to me. That thinking permeates a lot of society today. The younger generations aren't into being loyal to the company or its leadership. I find them being loyal to only themselves. They aren't after huge pensions; they are after a lifestyle they desire. They are more into living in the now than preparing for the future. Unfortunately, I think that may bite them later on in life. Nonetheless, I write that just to show you that as a leader you have to be loyal to all levels, even when others aren't. A leader's loyalty isn't based upon the unstable emotions and feeling of others. It is a decision that was made long before they were in the position of leadership. Perhaps it was the upbringing their parents gave them or perhaps they developed it out of a sense of duty. Either way, it is a necessary trait and characteristic a leader has in their foundation. It girds up all the other values. Loyalty knows very few boundaries. A leader doesn't blindly give loyalty. The leader is only loyal as long as the ethical boundaries and reciprocity is in order. Reciprocity means that the loyalty should come full circle. As a leader exhibits loyalty, it should always come back to them. It's when it quits coming back that either the culture or the leader is due for change. Either way a change is in order. Enron is an example of this. The loyalty of the leadership wasn't to the organization and people and today it is no longer in existence. Many people lost huge retirement benefits and pensions because leadership was missing the foundational girding of loyalty. Don't ever let that be said of you.

Chapter 24
LEADERS ARE GIVERS, NOT TAKERS

"Givers have to set limits because takers rarely do."
—Irma Kurtz

I don't expect this chapter to be a popular chapter. I am not suggesting that leaders should take a low level of compensation when they are responsible and capable of bringing organizations to a high level of success and sustainability. This chapter has more to do with an attitude leaders need to develop. I have seen too many leaders come into organizations that were healthy and profitable only to sell off the stock, reap a huge windfall, and then leave the company and its people nearly penniless or even worse, bankrupt. Being appointed to top leadership positions in an organization is an honor and an obligation that a leader should take very seriously. The leader should adopt an attitude that they are there to give the best they have to the community, the organization, and the board members, or whomever they are there to serve, other than themself. Leaders look for ways to give. They love to give as they live to give. Leadership in organizations places unreal demands upon leaders of all types and levels. Leaders recognize this and make the changes necessary to ensure they are seen as the givers they need to be. I don't believe any leader should blindly give. That could cause any leader to end up emotionally and financially bankrupt. No one can afford to be that way or live that way. Being a giver is simply a way of life that comes from the mindset the leader has developed.

We all heard it in President John F. Kennedy's speech of, "Don't ask what your country can do for you, but rather, what you can do for your country."

Leaders realize it isn't all about them. It is about the people they are working for. I despise the times I was in organizations where I found the leadership thinking everyone was there for them and not the other way around. They were takers not givers. I actually wonder how they slept at night being so selfish and self-centered. Being a giver is placing yourself in a position to be the lender instead of the borrower. It places expectations of reliability upon you as a leader that everyone around you knows what to expect. I often found that many givers are also very good receivers. They like being recognized for their giving but not always because they gave. They enjoy allowing others to be recognized with them. It isn't always about them. It is about those they serve through their giving. Leaders don't just give financially. Their giving radiates in every area of their life. Be honest with yourself and ask whether you as a leader are a giver or a taker. Take the necessary action to become a giver. The best leaders I have ever met were givers. Will you and I be seen as one?Only we can answer that and change our direction in positive ways. Be determined to be a giver.

Chapter 25
LEADERS LEARNED THE HARD WAY AND ISSUES OTHERS WON'T ADDRESS

"Follow the path of the unsafe, independent thinker. Expose your ideas to the dangers of controversy. Speak your mind and fear less the label of 'crackpot' than the stigma of conformity. And on issues that seem important to you, stand up and be counted at any cost."—Thomas J. Watson

This chapter isn't one I was looking forward to writing. Nonetheless, I believe it is necessary in keeping with my philosophy of being open and forthcoming. I want to mention a couple of lessons that I know can keep you from harming your career. One is anger. I see people today who wear anger on their sleeves. I see it in their eyes. They wake up angry and they go to sleep angry. The reasons are as varied as the numerous people in which I have witnessed it. The problem is when we allow anger to be manifested through our actions. I have seen managers blow it with anger. It's usually not until it's too late that the damage has been done. The immaturity or unwise decision was allowed to play forth. It doesn't matter the reason a Leader allows it to happen or even if the Leader can justify it. It is wrong. Psalm 37:8b states, "Do not lose your temper, it only leads to harm." Or how about Proverb 12:16, "A fool is quick tempered, but a wise person stays calm when insulted." Or Proverbs 13:10, "Pride leads to conflict; those who take advice are wise." I have never had anything good come from losing my temper. I am fortunate to have used much self-control and manifested anger very little. However, the times I have, left me embarrassed and excuseless. It doesn't matter whether I can justify it or not. It is wrong. A two year old can lose their temper. I know we are only human and susceptible to failure in any area. This is an area that I kicked myself about because I had allowed myself to be sucked in and then I allowed the fireworks to fly. Sure, I could excuse it away. I was provoked. However, I am not a victim. I am in control of my emotions and myself.

As a leader, I have a higher standard I have set for myself. I don't just follow standards; I set them. Therefore, when I fail I don't take it very well. My rule of thumb is that if one feels they are about to lose it, they need to leave the room, take a deep breath, get some perspective, and cool off. Manifesting anger when provoked is too easy. In today's society we are challenged on every front and pride plays a major role in contributing to the outcome we don't desire. I beg and implore you to get counseling if this is an area with which you are struggling. It isn't a weakness for you to learn to control your emotions, and the pay off will be major in your life and your career.

Another area to watch is being proper with those of the opposite sex. I haven't fallen into wrong temptation with this; however, others may have motives we all have to watch out for. I don't care what television shows us on prime time about male and female office relationships. Television doesn't show us reality. Television shows us only what the producers want us to see. It is scripted. Life isn't as scripted as that. Everyone must be on their guard to be as appropriate as the culture determines is acceptable. You still have to look yourself in the mirror each morning and evening. Make sure you are proud of what you see. You can say that you gave it your best shot. Remember, someone somewhere is proud of you. Your parents, wife, husband, children, teachers, and the lists go on. Don't do things to bring shame on yourself and them. Have the integrity to show others that the same person in private is the same person in public. You can be counted on to do the right things at the right times. We all have done things we are less than proud of, let's leave them in the past, and keep walking into our future.

I also want to mention that if you have failed, it doesn't necessarily mean disqualification. I don't like how society discards heroes and others when they fail. Have you ever met anyone alive who hasn't had a failure at something? I can't. If you want to tell me you have never failed, don't bother. Sell that line to someone else. There seems to be a double standard at times when we don't allow others to fail, but we do allow it for ourselves. If and when you do fail, don't beat yourself up too much about it. Learn from it and move on. We can't change the past but we can direct our future. Don't allow others to box you in with your failure. As a leader just own it and move on. Yes, it is as simple as that. We don't need to serve a penance and suffer. I find that most of the time the hardest person to forgive is myself. I have set up such high expectations that I honestly wonder who could possibly live up to them. I am in the health-care field. I practiced as an ED Nurse in an area where you aren't allowed to make mistakes or people die. Society doesn't allow failure from their favorite NFL teams and they boo their quarterback for being inconsistent. Inconsistency will cost all of us. Learn from mistakes, forgive yourself, and move on. My failures do not define me and neither do my successes. I am too big an entity in this universe to be defined by my one moment in time. I have a bunch of moments in time as a Father, Husband, Professional, Friend, Colleague, and Faith. You should desire the same.

Another area I find to be a landmine is arrogance. No one is so perfect they should be able to run up the flagpole for everyone to see. I find that arrogant people are hiding insecurities. I especially see this in leaders. I think one has to take a step back if your self-esteem comes from the position you are in and not the person you are. It took me years to learn that. I thought I was a "somebody" in a position, when in reality I was just another person to whom God had granted a great life. It wasn't me, it was God who allowed me the favor to become and to be. Once I could acknowledge that, at least I could see he loved me enough to make a difference in my life. No more arrogance. Stop reading your own press clippings and for goodness sake, stop thinking more of yourself than necessary. People run from arrogant people for fear they will be embarrassed or humiliated. Develop a little humility and watch people want to be close to you.

To summarize, I think we all know those things that make us stumble. Don't allow them to be landmines set up to trap you. Recognize them and avoid them. Place yourself in a position to be successful. Live with success and limit regret. We are human and we make mistakes but we don't allow mistakes or failures to become the things in this life that define us. Be wise. Seek wisdom.

FINAL WORDS

"I finally figured out the only reason to be alive is to enjoy it."
—*Rita Mae Brown, US author and social activist*

This chapter is for some simple thoughts and pleasures. Thank you for taking your valuable time to read my book and writings. I never underestimate how important people are in my life. I can't wait to meet people I have never met and to learn from them as well as keep investing in them. Enjoy my book and use the lessons for your own success. Leaders learn from everything they do. They are constantly observing. Look for lessons in everything you do. Look for lessons to learn. Don't ever think you know it all. Life and business will pass you by.

- Embrace the changes necessary for success. They may be painful but they are definitely worth the price paid.
- Subject yourself to the disciplines of life and live.
- Don't look for easy street—It doesn't exist.
- Don't fear. Control the emotions.
- Shaken Not Taken! Your confidence may be shaken, but don't ever let it be taken.
- Invest in Others. People are our greatest resource and investment.
- Read, Read and then Read some more!

- Have Fun!
- Live Each New Day as though it's your Last.
- Always Smile.

I pray for your success!It will be OK!

Your Friend and Author,
Howard Lull

AN OVERVIEW

Leaders Is Learned
- Observing
- Experimenting
- Questioning
- Grasping
- Lifetime of Learning

Leaders Is Imparted
- People don't care how much you know until they know how much you care.
- Constant reminder: It's all about people
- Imparting is an active exercise
- Understand: It's not about the Leader
- Understand: It's about the people you lead
- Tom Landry: "I just get people to do what they don't want to do, in order to achieve what it is they desire."
- Leaders Learn Loyalty and Love
- Leaders define a Vision
- In Healthcare: Cost, Service, Quality
- In Leadership: People, End Result, People
- Know who Imparts the Vision
- Know who carries out the Vision
- Lead the way—Get out of the way
- Leaders are givers not takers
- Leaders Have a Presence
- A Leader has a spirit of knowing who they are and what they are supposed to be doing

- A Leader has a presence amongst the people or group they are leading
- Leaders are born for certain times.
- Leaders develop and accept Personal Accountability—Excuses Embarrass Leaders
- Leaders offer No excuses—They fix the problem
- Leaders have developed Intangibles
- There are qualities a Leader possesses that cannot be seen by the naked eye.
- You know they have IT, but you can't always define what IT is.
- Intangibles: Confidence, Calm, Cool under pressure, Temperament, Excellence, You desire to follow or be a part of the direction they are heading
- Attitude: Baggage best left at the door. No room for it because it takes up space you need for other things.

Leaders work themselves out of a job
- In a good way!
- Things work when the Leader isn't there.
- It's not a false pride or a recognition thing, leaders don't need it.
- There is a difference in being in charge "responsible" and being accountable
- Let those who need to do their thing, do it. Get out of the way. Don't mess it up.

Leaders Exhibit Self-Control
- Emotions are disciplined.
- No good thing has ever come from fear and intimidation.
- Time is scheduled. There is a reason for all you do
- Roger's Rules for Success: "Never let your dress be second guessed."
- Do not draw attention to themselves, but to the end result.
- Let their Yes be Yes and their No be No.

Leaders know it's about what they SEE and HEAR
- What do you see?
- Can you see it before it ever materializes?
- What do you hear?
- Many voices pulling at you, often demanding
- If you can't SEE it or HEAR it, you can't have it.

Leaders have followers
- Leaders must also be followers
- Following is not a weakness. It is a Choice!
- Leaders give respect to followers
- Why would I follow me?
- Leaders extend mercy not judgment to followers
- Leaders don't allow people to confuse being nice with being weak
- Leaders hold themselves accountable
- Leaders allow themselves to be **VULNERABLE**

Leaders are Servants
- Learn to serve
- Being a servant is not the same as being a slave
- One is a choice the other is not
- Leaders do not "Deserve" to be Leaders
- Leaders Make themselves Leaders and are **Called**
- Leaders do not become too casual with others—it diminishes their effectiveness

Helpful Hints
- Learn from everything you do.
- Look for lessons to learn
- Subject yourself to the disciplines
- Embrace Change
- Don't look for easy street—It doesn't exist
- Do not fear
- Your confidence may be shaken—But don't ever let it be taken. "Shaken not Taken."
- Leaders perform honest self assessments

- Leaders know their weaknesses or areas for improvement better than anyone else
- Leaders surround themselves with strong people
- Leaders let go of insecurities—they don't carry a security blanket
- It's not what you see that will cause you trouble, It's what you don't see.
- A Leader makes those around them better.
- The Leader raises the level of professionalism and service by raising the level of expectations.
- Raising the level of expectation requires raising the level of thinking.
- Leaders hold themselves and others accountable for achieving the expectations.

Leaders Take Risk
- Leaders give themselves and others permission to succeed.
- Leaders give themselves and others permission to fail.
- A Leader does not allow success or failure to define them.
- A Leader seeks new horizons when the old ones have been conquered.
- Leaders aim higher than the stated goal.
- Leaders understand: It will be OK!
- Leaders develop and establish cultures of caring.
- Cultures define acceptable behaviors and expectations.
- An established culture allows people to feel secure, secure people produce quality work.
- Leaders create high quality environments.
- Leaders make those around them better.
- This is done by preparation.
- Leaders cannot change anyone—they can only influence them.
- Establish a value of embracing change.
- To be destined for success—you must embrace the disciplines.
- Embracing disciplines improves effectiveness.
- Leaders expect opposition.

- Leaders respond instead of reacting.
- One is a choice the other is a reflex.
- Leaders that react are often embarrassed and wrong.
- Take the time to think before responding.
- You aren't obligated to respond if you aren't prepared to respond.
- Leaders have a personal plan.
- Take the time to invest in and renew yourself.
- Dr Robert Schuller: "If it's going to be—it's up to me!"
- Answer your own questions—hire a coach if necessary and read, read, read!
- Leaders give and give and often deplete themselves before they realize they are depleted.

Final Words
- The rule is: "There aren't any rules!"
- That's not a license to be illegal!
- Actively throw off any self imposed limitations
- Establish new standards.
- Run "IT" Don't let "IT" run you!
- Have Fun! Enjoy Life! Enjoy Others!

NOTES OF YOUR LESSONS LEARNED

HOWARD LULL

HOWARD LULL

HOWARD LULL

HOWARD LULL

www.ingramcontent.com/pod-product-compliance
Lightning Source LLC
Chambersburg PA
CBHW021446210526
45463CB00002B/647